PECOS BILL

A TALL TALE RETOLD AND ILLUSTRATED BY

STEVEN KELLOGG

MORROW JUNIOR BOOKS • NEW YORK

Library of Congress Cataloging in Publication Data
Kellogg, Steven. Pecos Bill. Summary: Incidents from the life of Pecos Bill, from his childhood among the coyotes to his unusual wedding day. 1. Pecos Bill (Legendary character)—Juvenile literature. [1. Pecos Bill (Legendary character) 2. Folklore—United States. 3. Tall tales.]
I. Title. PZ8.1K3Pe 1986 398.2'2'09764 86-784   10 9 8 7 6   First Mulberry Edition, 1992   ISBN 0-688-09924-6

To Jason Castle Edwards—Another Texas Hero

Back in the rugged pioneer days when Pecos Bill was a baby, his kinfolk decided that New England was becoming entirely too crowded, so they piled into covered wagons and headed west.

The clan considered settling in East Texas, until Bill's ma noticed a homesteader putting up a shack about fifty miles away. "Another crowded neighborhood," she grumbled. "Let's push on."

As they crossed the Pecos River, Bill threw out a fishing line. But when a Texas trout nibbled, Bill was yanked overboard.

He was towed far downstream, and he would've drowned for sure if an old coyote hadn't grabbed him.

Her family adopted Bill and taught him the ways of wild creatures.

By the time Bill had outgrown his breeches, he felt like a member of the pack.

He loved to romp with his coyote brothers, and as he grew older, he sometimes played with the bighorn sheep.

One day a drifter named Chuck stumbled across Bill while he was taking a nap.

He asked Bill what he meant by snoozing in the brush without his trousers. Bill tried to explain that he was a coyote.

"Horsefeathers!" said Chuck. "You're a Texan, just like me."

Bill decided to give life as a Texan a try. He borrowed
Chuck's extra clothes and peppered him with questions.

"To tell you the truth," said Chuck, "most Texans are flea-bitten outlaws, and the worst of them are the Hell's Gulch Gang. But even they would be okay if they'd become ranchers and herd the longhorns that wander hereabouts."

Ranching sounded good to Bill, and he headed for Hell's Gulch, determined to recruit the Gang.

But Bill's plans were interrupted when he was ambushed
by a giant rattlesnake.

When Bill dodged the snake's fangs, it slapped its coils around him.

The snake squeezed hard, but Bill squeezed harder and he didn't let up until every drop of poison was out of that reptile, leaving it skinny as a rope and mild as a goldfish.

Then, before Bill could catch his breath, he was tackled by a critter that was part grizzly, part puma, part gorilla, and part tarantula. They wrestled up and down the canyon and kicked up quite a dust storm before the monster finally became so dizzy it had to quit.

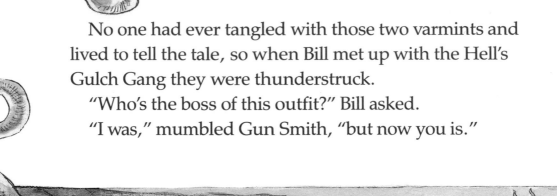

No one had ever tangled with those two varmints and lived to tell the tale, so when Bill met up with the Hell's Gulch Gang they were thunderstruck.

"Who's the boss of this outfit?" Bill asked.

"I was," mumbled Gun Smith, "but now you is."

Bill told the gang that he was going to turn every last one of them into respectable ranch hands. But the men claimed that Texas cattle were much too ornery to ever put up with ranching.

Bill had a sudden inspiration, and he approached a longhorn that was sulking nearby.

Just as the bull whirled around to trample him, Bill snagged him with the rattlesnake and yanked with all his might. "Cattle roping has just been invented!"

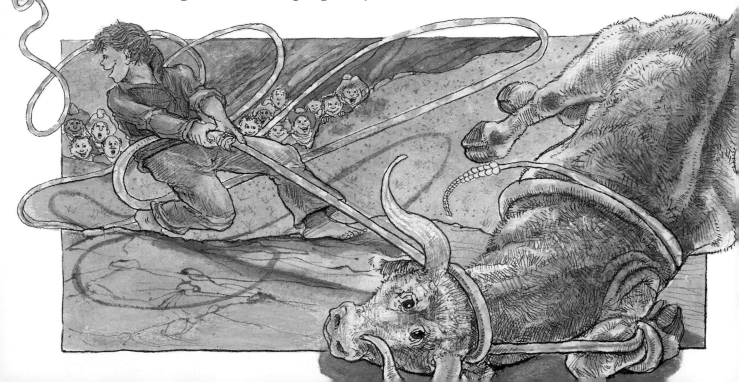

Bill scared that bull out of its skin with a blood-curdling coyote howl. The embarrassed creature hightailed it off to grow a new coat, while Bill cut the hide into strips and passed them out to the men to use as lassos.

Then cowboys and cattle tangled in a rough and tumble hullaballoo that is remembered to this day as the first western rodeo.

When it ended, the Gang declared they would be cowboys forever, and they promised to help Bill round up every steer in Texas.

Bill needed a horse to ride on the big roundup. "Well," said Chuck, "there's a wild stallion in the mountains that some folks call Lightning. Others think the name Widow-maker suits him better. But no matter what you call him, he's the fastest, most beautiful horse in the world."

Bill went off in search of Lightning. As soon as he saw him, Bill knew he'd found the horse for him.

Bill chased Lightning north to the Arctic Circle...

and south to the bottom of the Grand Canyon.

Finally he cornered the stallion and jumped onto his back. Lightning exploded from the canyon, leaping and bucking across three states.

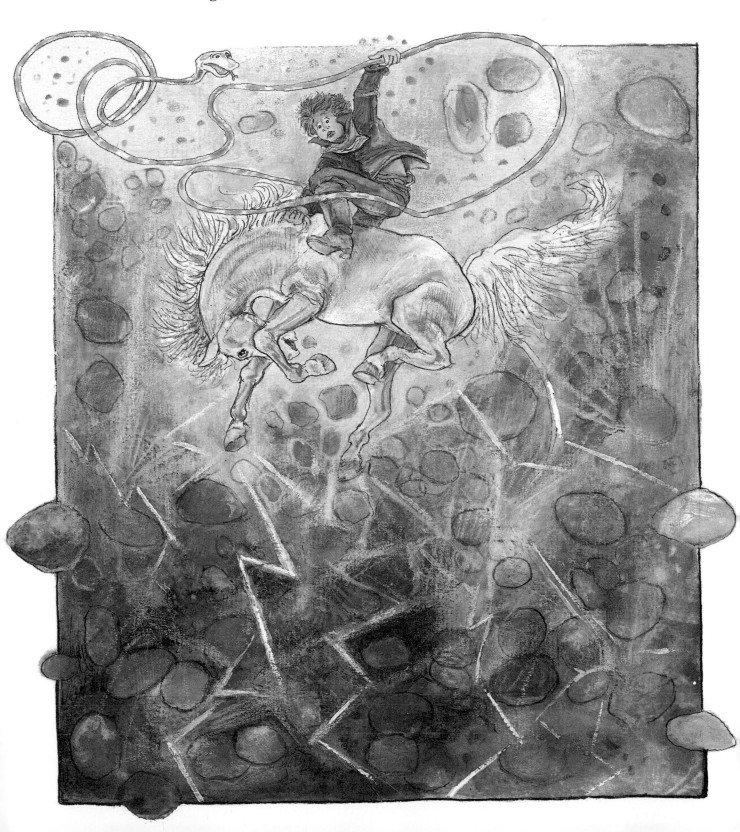

Then Bill began to sing in the language he had learned from his coyote family. He sang of his admiration for the stallion's strength and promised him a lifetime of partnership and devotion.

When Bill was done singing, he offered the horse his freedom, but Lightning chose to follow him forever.

With Pecos Bill and Lightning leading them, the cowboys whooped across the state of Texas, rounding up every last steer. But their high spirits collapsed when they were faced with the job of driving that enormous herd back and forth between the summer and winter ranges.

To silence their grumbling, Bill set up the Perpetual Motion Ranch on Pinnacle Peak, which was so high that the top remained in winter while spring and autumn turned into summer at the base.

A team of prairie dogs helped Bill to fence off the mountain so that the cattle could wander through the seasons unattended.

Bill's plan worked fine except that Pinnacle Peak was so steep the steers fell right off whenever there was a breeze. The men had to work harder than ever carrying the cattle back up the hill.

Bill solved that problem by inventing steers with very short legs on one side of their bodies. Even in a windstorm these cattle could stand securely on the slope as long as they kept their short-legged sides uphill.

Now the men at Perpetual Motion Ranch had all kinds of free time, and Bill became known as the world's greatest cowboy.

But the high point of Bill's life came when Slewfoot Sue passed by on the back of a catfish. Bill was instantly in love and he hollered a proposal of marriage.

Sue agreed, on two conditions: first, Bill had to buy her a wedding dress with a bustle, and second, he had to let her ride Lightning to the ceremony.

The first request was easy. Bill galloped to Dallas and brought back the fanciest bustled dress in the city.

Sue's second request was not so simple.

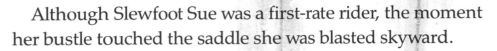

Although Slewfoot Sue was a first-rate rider, the moment
her bustle touched the saddle she was blasted skyward.

Sue soared around the moon and began the long descent
to earth.

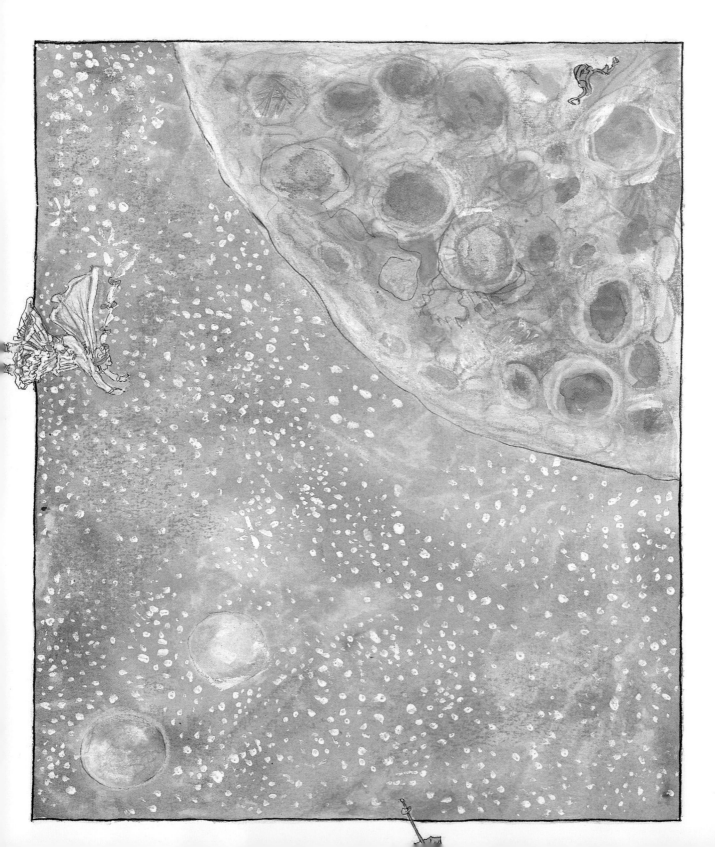

She landed squarely on her bustle, but quick as Bill was, he couldn't get to her before she bounced back into outer space.

Time and time again, Sue hit the ground and rocketed back toward the stars.

Sue probably would have sailed back and forth forever if Bill hadn't lassoed a tornado to help him catch his bouncing bride.

The pair of them clung to that careening storm until it blew itself out over California. To Bill's amazement, he and Sue landed on top of his ma and pa's wagon.

Bill couldn't believe his kinfolk were still searching for a homesite. He told them they could spend the rest of their days roaming but they'd never find a place to equal Texas.

Everyone returned to Bill's ranch for a wingding of a family reunion. And today their descendants are still there, happily herding cattle.